pilgrim

LEADER'S GUIDE
A COURSE FOR THE CHRISTIAN JOURNEY

The Authors

Stephen Cottrell is the Bishop of Chelmsford
Steven Croft is the Bishop of Sheffield
Paula Gooder is a leading New Testament writer and lecturer
Robert Atwell is the Bishop of Stockport

pilgrim

LEADER'S GUIDE
A COURSE FOR THE CHRISTIAN JOURNEY

STEPHEN COTTRELL
STEVEN CROFT
PAULA GOODER
ROBERT ATWELL

THE CHURCH
OF ENGLAND

CHURCH HOUSE
PUBLISHING

Church House Publishing
Church House
Great Smith Street
London SW1P 3AZ

ISBN 978 0 7151 4378 0

Published 2013 by Church House Publishing

Cover and contents design by David McNeill, Revo Design.

Printed in Great Britain by
Ashford Colour Press Ltd

CONTENTS

pilgrim

Preface
by the Archbishops of Canterbury and York

One of the most significant developments in the Church in recent years is the rediscovery that, for most people, becoming a Christian is like a journey, and that the local church can best help people make that journey by providing opportunity and resources for catechesis and discipleship.

Pilgrim is a course for the Christian journey. It encourages every church to think about developing a place where those who are not yet Christians can come and find out about the Christian faith, and experience Christian community. In this way *Pilgrim* enables people to encounter Christ and receive and engage with the teaching of the Church.

In the Early Church this process of evangelism and catechesis was called a catechumenate. The teaching of the Christian faith was based around the learning and receiving of key texts which summed up and communicated the heart of the Christian message, texts like the Apostles' Creed, the Ten Commandments, the Lord's Prayer and the Beatitudes.

Pilgrim aims to be a catechumenate for today's Church of England. Like our forebears it bases its communication of the Christian faith around these basic texts. It also offers for the wider teaching of the Christian faith a slightly adapted version of *A Revised Catechism*.

Learning about the Christian faith means learning about God. This is not the sort of knowledge that can simply be extracted from a book. We can only know God by entering into that relationship with God that is made possible by the life, death and resurrection of Jesus Christ. There is learning to be done, but it is primarily about a relationship. That is why, in *Pilgrim*, time is spent in fellowship, reflective Bible reading and prayer as much as discussion. In this way those who are exploring the Christian faith are formed as a little community of faith, learning and praying together as they seek the way of Christ. And the only qualification needed to be part of a *Pilgrim* group is to want to find out more.

It is hoped that this simple approach to sharing the Christian faith will be a real encouragement to churches who have not yet engaged in this sort of ministry, or who have found other resources less appropriate for their situation, or who are just looking for something new. It is an initiative of the House of Bishops, and it is written by bishops in the Church of England and other leading theologians, men and women, but it is offered to the whole Church of God in this land.

In Scripture and tradition the journey of faith is often referred to as a pilgrimage. A pilgrimage is a journey to a holy place. The *Pilgrim* course is a journey to the heart of God and to a living, personal relationship with Jesus Christ within the household of his Church. It is offered to the parishes and communities of the Church of England that we might take more seriously the Great Commission to make disciples, and build in each of our parishes a place where people can come to know Christ and follow in the way of faith.

+Justin Cantuar:

+Sentamu Ebor:

pilgrim

PART ONE:
WELCOME TO *PILGRIM*

An Overview

Pilgrim is a course for the Christian journey. The aim of the course is to help people become disciples of Jesus Christ.

A pilgrim is a person on a journey. The Bible is a book full of journeys. God's people are always travelling. God's call to Abraham was to leave his own land for a great journey of faith. God's call to Moses was to lead God's people on a journey from slavery in Egypt to freedom in the promised land. Jesus took his first disciples on a journey from Galilee to Jerusalem. One of the earliest names for the people called Christians was followers of the Way.

Pilgrim is designed to help every local church to invite others to join the people of God on our great journey of faith. Its purpose is to help you to draw together a small group of people who are enquiring about Christian faith or are new to faith and to help them learn about the faith together.

This leader's guide is for clergy and church leaders who are thinking about introducing *Pilgrim* into the life of their church and is also a short handbook for those who will lead the groups.

The origins of *Pilgrim*

In 2010 the Church of England committed itself to three priorities for the present five-year period (or quinquennium):

● To grow the Church through the making of disciples

● To serve the common good of society

● To re-imagine ministry to enable us to do these two things better

The House of Bishops and the Archbishops' Council invited the authors in 2011 to develop new material to help the whole Church to grow through the making of disciples. *Pilgrim* is our response to that invitation.

The four lead authors are Robert Atwell, Stephen Cottrell, Steven Croft and Paula Gooder. We all bring different experiences of helping people to learn and grow in faith. *Pilgrim* has been developed in conversation with many other people and we have involved a wide range of bishops, clergy and lay people in writing the materials.

The structure of *Pilgrim*

There are many different aspects to helping people learn about the Christian faith.

We have taken as our starting point Jesus' summary of the commandments. We are called to offer our lives to God through loving God with all our mind, soul, strength and heart and to love our neighbour as ourselves. Learning about Christian faith and growing in Christian faith is about more than what we believe. It's also about the ways in which we pray and develop our relationship with God, about the way we live our lives and about living in God's vision for the Church and for the world.

We offer two stages of material in *Pilgrim*. There are four short *Pilgrim* books (each comprising a course of six sessions) in the 'Follow' Stage designed for those who are enquirers and very new to the faith. Then there are four short *Pilgrim* books (again, each comprising a six-session course) in the 'Grow' Stage designed for those who want to go further and learn more.

The structure of *Pilgrim* is set out in the diagram.

PILGRIM				
A Course for the Christian Journey				
	What do Christians believe?	How do Christians know and worship God?	How do Christians behave?	What is the Christian vision for the world?
FOLLOW STAGE *'Do you turn to Christ?'*	**❶** TURNING TO CHRIST	**❷** THE LORD'S PRAYER	**❸** THE COMMANDMENTS	**❹** THE BEATITUDES
GROW STAGE *'Will you continue in the Apostles' teaching and fellowship?'*	**❺** THE CREEDS	**❻** THE EUCHARIST	**❼** THE BIBLE	**❽** CHURCH AND KINGDOM
	Doctrine	Spirituality	Ethics	Lifestyle

Each short course consists of six sessions. The courses in the Follow Stage are designed to be led by someone who is further on in their Christian faith and who is a skilled teacher. The courses in the Grow Stage are designed so that the group can lead and guide themselves with some external help and support.

In the Follow Stage, each of the four courses is structured around one of four key texts:

● the credal questions asked before Baptism

● the Lord's Prayer

● the Commandments

● the Beatitudes.

These four texts have been important in helping people in the early stages of their Christian journey since the earliest days of the Christian faith.

In the Grow Stage, each of the four courses is structured around a major theme of the Christian life:

● the Creeds

● the Sacraments

● the Scriptures

● living in God's Church and in God's world.

Each session of each course is rooted in shared prayer. Each session begins with the group exploring the Scriptures together and continues with a more sustained reflection on the theme and opportunity for questions and discussion.

There is a *Pilgrim* website (www.pilgrimcourse.org) which contains resources to support those using the course, including sound files of the Reflections included in each session, short videos to introduce the sessions and other support materials.

It is strongly recommended that you sign up to the email news facility on the site to make sure you are kept informed as to when new components of the course and new support materials are made available online, etc.

The short courses in the four Follow Stage books can be approached in any order. Together, we believe they offer a balanced introduction to the Christian life and journey. Our hope and prayer is that *Pilgrim* will help to introduce people to the Christian Way and also equip them to live their whole lives as disciples of Jesus Christ.

About this Leader's Guide

This guide is both an introduction to *Pilgrim* and a guide to using it well. The next section, Part Two: Teaching the Faith, explores some of the ideas behind the course and the principles that have guided its development. Part Three: Leading a *Pilgrim* Group is a more practical guide to gathering and leading a group on one or more short courses. Part Four: Pilgrim Resources gives details of the various books and publication dates, the website and other resources. Finally, Part Five offers some powerful images and an understanding of the role of the teacher, the group leader and catechist in this process of making new disciples.

pilgrim

PART TWO:
TEACHING THE FAITH

Catechesis

Catechesis is a word used throughout Christian history for special teaching offered to Christians who are preparing for baptism or who are newly baptized. It's an unfamiliar word to most people today but well worth learning. It is pronounced KAT-ER-KEY-SIS.

It is Luke who first uses the term *catechesis* to describe the special teaching given to new Christians. Luke dedicates his gospel to Theophilus:

> so that you may know the truth concerning the things about which you have been instructed [literally, *catechized*].
>
> LUKE 1.4

In Acts, Luke introduces Apollos as someone who had been 'instructed [literally, catechized] in the way of the Lord' (Acts 18.25), though he remained in need of further teaching.

Much of the New Testament, including the gospels, was written to support this great work of catechesis, the early instruction of new disciples both before and immediately after their baptism. Many of the early creeds and formulas we know from the New Testament were also developed to support this work of teaching the faith to those who were learning it for the first time.

In the early centuries of the Christian faith, the gospel spread and the Church grew in a context that was often hostile and difficult. It was a costly thing to be a Christian. Careful preparation and support was essential both before and after baptism. The Early Church therefore developed ways of teaching the faith and making disciples centred on preparation for baptism and gave this work the name of the catechumenate. Many of the great traditions of the Christian Church began as a way of supporting those who were learning the faith for the first time. In particular, the season of Lent was originally a time of preparation for baptism at Easter, kept by the whole Church in support of the candidates.

The catechism

All down the centuries, in periods of mission and growth, the Church in every tradition has always paid particular attention to the task of catechesis and to *what* should be taught to new Christians in the form of the different *catechisms*.

A catechism is a way of the Church ensuring together that new Christians learn all that they need to learn in preparation for their baptism and for a lifetime of Christian discipleship.

Some catechisms are quite short and designed to be learned by heart. The Church of England has its own catechism, last revised in 1962 and last authorized by the General Synod in 1996. It is reproduced at the end of this book.

You will see that this authorized catechism is quite brief and in a question and answer form that is designed to be learned by heart. It contains not only a short statement of Christian belief, based on the Apostles' Creed, but also guidance on how Christians should live, based on the Ten Commandments and Jesus' summary of the law, an understanding of the Holy Spirit's work and sections on Worship and Prayer (based on the Lord's Prayer), Scripture, Sacraments and Ministries of Grace and the Christian Hope.

Some of the language of the present authorized catechism is dated or still in the forms found in the older liturgies of the Church of England, and 'man' and 'men' are used where we would now use the inclusive term 'person'. In parts the catechism clearly envisages that those learning it are children and young people who have been baptized in infancy and are preparing for confirmation. However, there are many strengths and much wisdom in the text as it stands. We have made some minor changes to the text to make the language inclusive and to include contemporary forms of the Commandments and the Lord's Prayer.

Other Church traditions have their own catechisms. The best known (and the longest) is the *Catechism of the Catholic Church*, first published in 1992 which runs to 700 pages in the standard English edition (Burns & Oates, 2000).

The *Catechism of the Catholic Church* has four sections:

1 The Creeds (the content or object of our faith based on the Nicene and Apostles' Creeds)

2 The Sacred Liturgy (how we celebrate and communicate the faith based around worship and an exposition of seven sacraments)

3 The Christian way of life (how we live out our faith based around the Commandments)

4 Christian Prayer (how we deepen our relationship with God based around the Lord's Prayer)

Unlike the *Catechism of the Church of England*, the *Catechism of the Catholic Church* is primarily intended as a guide for the whole Church in the great task of catechesis not as a manual to be placed in the hands of those learning the faith for the first time.

Why do we need new material?

In every generation, the Church needs to reflect on this great task of catechesis and the way in which we make disciples. This is especially true in seasons of significant renewal in the life of the Church or times of change in our wider society or periods of great missionary endeavour.

Many people would argue that the present time is one when the life of the Church of England needs to be renewed (and is being renewed) for the task we face. All would agree that we are living through times of great change in our society and the place of Christian faith within it. This is also a time when the Church is called to engage in God's mission, including the mission to make disciples, with fresh energy, creativity and zeal in the power of the Holy Spirit.

However, the Church is called to reflect on our methods and resources for catechesis, especially for the sake of the people in our own generation as we invite them to follow Jesus Christ and become his disciples.

The *Pilgrim* Way

We have tried to develop material that is suitable for catechesis in the twenty-first century in England. We believe there are ten distinctive characteristics.

Pilgrim starts at the very beginning

Many adults, children and young people who are open to exploring faith know very little about the faith when they begin that journey of exploration. For that reason, we need material that begins at the beginning, which assumes very little knowledge or understanding but simply a desire to learn and explore from first principles.

That means that for most people there is quite a lot to learn. We have prepared eight short courses. Four of them are for those starting out on the journey as enquirers and are called the Follow Stage of *Pilgrim*. The second group of four builds on the first and we have called this the Grow Stage.

A group could tackle the material in any order but it makes most sense to work through the Follow courses before the Grow material and for all groups to begin with the first course, *Turning to Christ*.

Pilgrim is about our whole lives

Living as a Christian is about more than simply believing a set of doctrines. Living as a disciple is about the whole of our lives. Much of the material currently used for teaching enquirers and new believers is fundamentally shaped by the Creeds. This element in catechesis is important. However, we believe our material needs to be balanced to help new disciples to pray and develop their relationship with God; to share fully in the life of the Church; and to live out their discipleship and ministry in the world. Catechesis needs to pay due attention to each of these aspects of the Christian life.

Each of these dimensions also needs to be reflected if possible in the life of the group. This means that, when the group meets, it will not simply be for study but will be about building community, praying together as faith grows, serving together and supporting one another in living out our discipleship.

Pilgrim focuses on following Jesus Christ

> At the heart of catechesis we find, in essence, a Person, the Person of Jesus of Nazareth, the only Son from the Father, who suffered and died for us and who now, after rising, is living with us forever. To catechize is to reveal in the Person of Christ the whole of God's eternal design reaching fulfilment in that Person.
>
> **CATECHISM OF THE CATHOLIC CHURCH**

Catechesis needs to be comprehensive but also clearly focused on equipping people to follow Jesus Christ as disciples in the whole of their lives. Catechesis is not a course in theology as an academic exercise. Catechesis is about being formed and shaped in the pattern of Christ and, in St Paul's words, about Christ being formed and shaped in us (Galatians 4.19).

A correct understanding is essential but cannot be divorced from a life that is being transformed and made whole and lived according to

God's call. Taking part in a *Pilgrim* group should lead to change both for the members of the group and for the leaders.

Pilgrim flows from the Scriptures

Christians believe that God has revealed himself to us in the Scriptures and supremely in the person of Jesus Christ, God's living Word, who is himself at the very heart of the Scriptures, God's written Word.

> All scripture is inspired by God (literally 'God-breathed') and is useful for teaching, for reproof, for correction and for training in righteousness so that everyone who belongs to God may be proficient and equipped for every good work.
>
> 2 TIMOTHY 3.16

Catechesis therefore needs to take the Scriptures seriously and introduce enquirers and new believers to a lifetime of engagement with the Scriptures through reading the Bible together. The primary focus of each session of *Pilgrim* is a group of people engaging together in reading the Bible and attending to Scripture together through careful reading of the text.

Some material for catechesis focuses simply on one part of Scripture, most commonly one of the gospels. However, it is important that a new Christian is helped to read, understand and interpret the whole of the Scriptures as part of the Church.

Through the different sections of the course we have introduced a range of different Scriptures, from both Old and New Testaments, from the gospels and the epistles and from the law, the prophets and the writings so that the participants begin to gain a rich, textured understanding of the Bible and learn to love reading the Scriptures as part of their discipleship.

Pilgrim draws deeply from the Christian tradition

In the United Kingdom in the twenty-first century we stand in a long tradition of catechesis which stretches back to the apostles. That tradition has much to teach us.

Pilgrim seeks to be faithful to that tradition in two ways. The first is by focusing on four key texts in the Follow Stage, and building on these in the Grow Stage. In the catechumenates of the Early Church these four texts were passed on and handed over (the root meaning of tradition) as a key part of preparation for baptism:

- **The Creeds** – the Baptismal creed is used in the Follow Stage and the Apostles' and Nicene Creeds in the Grow Stage.
- **The Lord's Prayer** – leading into the Eucharist in the Grow Stage.
- **The Commandments** – leading into the Scriptures in the Grow Stage.
- **The Beatitudes –** leading into a vision of the kingdom of God in the Grow Stage.

In addition, a whole range of authors from Christian history are included, with extracts, readings and prayers in each session giving a sense of the breadth and depth of Christian vision and providing a gateway to future learning and reflection.

Pilgrim honours the Anglican Way

Jesus Christ calls us not to solitary discipleship but to be disciples in community. Every disciple belongs to the one, holy, catholic and apostolic Church. However, we are also called to belong to a specific Church.

Over many centuries, the Holy Spirit has called and shaped the life of the Christian Churches in different ways. At the beginning of Christian discipleship it is more important to understand one way in depth, and to become part of that way, than to understand many different ways superficially.

Pilgrim is written to be a specifically Anglican resource which follows Anglican belief and practice at every point. We hope and pray that it will be useful to Anglicans beyond the Church of England in many other parts of the Anglican Communion. We trust that the material may be helpful to Christians of other traditions. However, we have not attempted to disguise who we are. *Pilgrim* is written in the hope that it will be used by God and by God's people to form disciples in an Anglican tradition of being Christian.

What this means will be seen more fully from the materials themselves. However, we would include as Anglican values that have shaped this material:

1 The importance of reading and engaging with the whole of Scripture in both Old and New Testaments

2 The valuing and balancing of Scripture, tradition, reason and experience in all reflection on faith and understanding

3 The teaching of the whole and historic Christian faith as summarized in the Apostles' and Nicene Creeds

4 Valuing especially the sacraments given by Jesus of the Eucharist and Baptism

5 The joys of liturgical worship inviting the participation of the whole people of God in the praise of his glory

6 A call to engage in God's mission to the whole of creation (as described in the Anglican Communion's five marks of mission)

7 A recognition that the whole people of God are called to discipleship and ministry each according to their gifts and vocation and to sharing in the governance and leadership of God's people

8   A recognition of the threefold order of deacon, priest and bishop in the ordering of the life of God's Church

9   A recognition that the outcome of discipleship and mission is community, social and cultural change around the world

10   A recognition of the importance of local culture in a global context for interpreting Scripture, discipleship and mission

Pilgrim helps people to learn in different ways

There are many different ways to help people learn about the Christian faith. We have set out in Learning the Faith some of the principles that have guided our own approach to teaching and learning in catechesis (pp. 32–7).

With the changing role of the Christian faith in our society, it seems particularly important to offer material and a method for catechesis which creates at the same time a level playing field between different members of a group and a community where people learn and grow together as partners in discipleship and as equals in faith.

In previous generations, Christian faith was commonly taught from a position of authority from an authorized and learned preacher or teacher imparting knowledge to (largely silent) students or learners. In our present context, such an approach is unlikely to be fruitful. Adult learning is now much more about active engagement and pooled experience and this is especially so in the area of faith.

Those who come to learn will almost certainly learn best in many different ways. A variety of approaches is vital in any single group. Anyone leading a group must be free to tailor the approach to their own particular group of learners. One of the tests of Christian faith is that the faith is seen to be authentic and lived out in the experience of those who teach. The group leaders therefore need to be willing to share themselves and their own experience and questions of faith in order to guide and lead the group well. The material provided for the group to work with must be flexible and adaptable to local need.

For this reason, the Scriptures are set out at the heart of *Pilgrim* as the primary teacher and source of reflection and instruction. Reading Scripture together and listening together to what the Spirit is saying to the Church creates a level playing field. It offers an experience where the whole group bring their insights, experience, questions and wisdom and learn together in community, initially with guidance from more experienced Christians.

Reading and reflection on Scripture together is followed in each session by a written reflection from one of a range of different voices in the Anglican tradition. Bishops and theologians contribute these essays to draw on a range of different sources and the whole rich variety of the Church of England.

The aim of these reflections is to help the group to learn individually and together about one or other aspect of the faith.

We hope the 'feel' of the group will be similar to other adult group learning experiences in contemporary society such as book groups, NCT classes, support groups or AA meetings.

Pilgrim helps disciples to go on learning for the whole of their lives

The best catechesis creates a lifelong appetite for learning about the Christian faith in many different ways. So we hope that each of the eight short courses in the material will create a thirst for the next and that the whole set of material will form and shape disciples who know that they have much more to learn, and commit to that continuous process of learning, growing and change throughout their lives.

Specifically, we envisage that the first four short courses in the Follow Stage of *Pilgrim* will be led by skilled group leaders who are trained and equipped to lead others in catechesis. However, we also hope that through these first four sections of the course each group will become a learning community and that new leaders will emerge who can guide the group through the Grow Stage of the course and on into further learning and life together into the future. *Follow* is therefore a tool not simply for the catechesis of individuals but for the formation of small mission-shaped Christian communities which are the building blocks of the life of the local church.

Pilgrim can be used by every tradition in the Church of England

The Church of England is a very diverse Church at the beginning of the twenty-first century. We gather in cathedrals and parish churches, in prisons, hospitals and schools, in many and various fresh expressions of the Church. There are many small communities. There are many large churches as well. Some meet in inner cities or outer estates. Others gather and serve suburban parishes or rural communities. Some churches are nurtured by one part of the Anglican tradition, others by another.

Our aim has been to provide material that can be used fruitfully in a very wide variety of settings. We don't think it will always be the best material for every situation. However, as authors we believe there will be real advantages in having good quality material which can be used across the different traditions and contexts of Church, in fresh expressions of Church and parishes, cathedrals and chaplaincies, and which is able to draw men and women and young people into a common experience of what it means to be a disciple of Jesus Christ in the Anglican tradition.

Pilgrim can be used with young people and adults

Our hope and prayer is that *Pilgrim* can be used effectively with groups of young people as well as with adult groups (or with groups that mix the two). However, some additional adaptation might be needed when working with younger teenagers.

Pilgrim is realistic in its use of resources

Some churches are outwardly rich in resources for catechesis, and others are, on the surface, less well off. Resources include finances for materials, premises to meet in, and most of all people available to help lead and support the life of the nurture groups.

Pilgrim has been designed to serve a variety of contexts and especially those where there are outwardly few resources. All you need is a copy of the course book for each person; a copy of this leader's guide for the group leaders, a room to meet in and some light refreshments. You can, of course add things as you have them (such as a television to show the DVDs, a meal together, a retreat or day away), but these are not essential.

If even these resources seem beyond your church we would encourage you to look at two things carefully.

The first is to explore again your understanding of God's grace and the rich gifts of ministry God gives to the Church. There are many instances in the Bible of God's people having very few resources, but God providing all that is needed and more as people move forward in faith. The story of the feeding of the multitude in John 6 is a good place to begin. What are five barley loaves and two fish among so many? Give thanks for what you have, pray and believe and be surprised at what God will provide.

The second is to review your priorities individually and as a church. Where are the time, energy and resources going if you do not have the time and resources as a parish church of the Church of England to offer one opportunity each year for new people to learn more about the Christian faith? In many parishes, a situation has become so normal which is in reality a scandal.

Read and teach the gospels again and especially be alert to the priority Jesus gives to those who are lost. Luke 15 is a good place to begin. Ask yourself what priorities Jesus would set for the Church. Then take action together.

An Annual Rhythm

As mentioned above, the Church of England has committed itself in the coming years to grow the Body of Christ in both numbers and in depth of discipleship. It is vital to recognize the importance of catechesis in this task of growing the Church.

In all of our talk about mission action planning and strategies for growth there is one key critical event. That critical event takes place when lay or ordained ministers gather a small group of people who are enquiring about the Christian faith and want to learn more. The group may be just two or three people or a dozen. Together the group journeys and explores the Christian gospel in such a way that people are able to make a response of faith and become Christians and they move on to be established and equipped as disciples.

Where this critical event is happening over and over again in a regular cycle, there will be people in your church coming to faith and growing in faith. Where that is happening the church is likely to be growing in numbers and depth of service. But where this critical event of catechesis is not happening, no amount of strategy and planning for ministry can replace it. A refocusing of the energy of lay and ordained ministers on ministry catechesis is absolutely vital for the growth of the Church in the twenty-first century.

It doesn't matter whether the church in question is urban or rural, a cathedral or a fresh expression of church. For the church to be growing there must be an intentional focusing of time and energy in the ministry of catechesis.

The importance of this work is borne out in a number of studies where only one significant common factor has emerged so far in relation to spiritual and numerical growth in parishes: the frequency of offering nurture groups (which is at the heart of catechesis). It is no coincidence that the same factor is highly significant in the overall morale and role satisfaction of the clergy.

But how can catechesis become more central in the ordinary life of every Anglican parish and fresh expression of Church in the present day? There are many competing demands on time and energy. One answer is to return to first principles and to begin to make good use again of the cycle of the Christian year.

The diagram below shows one way of doing this which we want to commend. The year is divided into three seasons, using the agricultural picture that is common in the gospels and in Paul's writings (see Matthew 13 and 1 Corinthians 3.5–9).

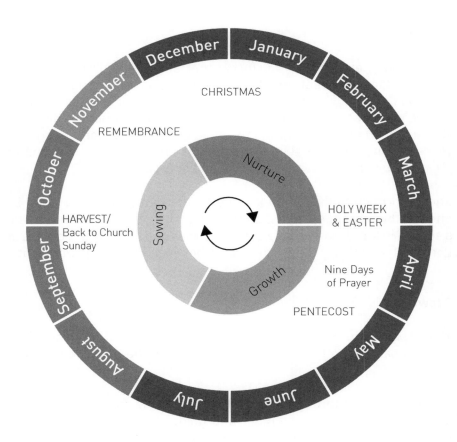

Sowing

The season of sowing the seed of the gospel outside of the life of the church from the summer through to mid autumn. There are many different ways in which this can be done through holiday clubs and activities for all ages; through Harvest Festivals and Back to Church Sunday; through ministry with families bringing children to baptism, coming to be married and through work with the bereaved throughout the year; through special outreach events or a regular programme of visiting.

Nurture

The season set aside for nurturing the faith of enquirers and new Christians from mid autumn through to Lent and leading up to Easter. Lent was originally a time of intense preparation for baptism for new adult candidates. This is the time of year to draw together the different contacts made through sowing the seed of the gospel throughout the year into one (or several) nurture groups. The first four sections of *Pilgrim* are designed for exactly this kind of group.

Each short course is six weeks long so the material can be used by offering the first course to the group in the six weeks before Christmas, a second in the six weeks between Christmas and Lent, a third course in Lent itself and finally the fourth course between Easter and Pentecost.

Growth

Third, every church community needs to offer ways in which every disciple can continue to grow and develop and be stretched in their faith.

This may happen through the creation of ongoing small communities of faith which continue to meet and guide themselves through the Discipleship material and thereafter use other material for their learning and growth. Or it may happen through the offering of times of learning for the whole church family outside of Sunday worship between Easter or Pentecost and the summer. These might include study days, retreats, parish pilgrimages or weekends away.

Prayer

Finally, this whole pattern of catechesis needs to be rooted and grounded in the prayer of the whole people of God. One helpful way to focus this is to use the nine days between Ascension and Pentecost each year as a nine-day (or novena) period of prayer especially for the making of disciples and the growth of the Church.

The Church of England is in the midst of a profound transition to become once again a Church in mission, making disciples as a normal and natural part of our common life. A key part of this transition is relearning this deep rhythm of catechesis, and setting that rhythm at the heart of our common life together so that every local Christian community sees itself again as a school for the Lord's service, a place where disciples are made and a community where people regularly find faith in Jesus Christ. A key task of lay and ordained ministers (but especially the ordained) is to lead this work of catechesis and ensure that this rhythm of teaching the faith grows and deepens with the years.

In many places, these core disciplines of sowing the seed of the gospel, nurturing the faith of enquirers and new believers and teaching the whole people of God are alive and well. These are the places where the Church of England is healthy and growing. In many other places, these disciplines have been sorely neglected and urgently need to be revived and practised by the whole people of God until they become again a normal and natural part of church life. Beginning to work with *Pilgrim* is a way of re-engaging with these core disciplines, which need to be present in every community.

The sequence is never neat or exact, of course. In the last analysis it doesn't really matter whether you offer your nurture group in October or May. It is unlikely that in any given year an individual would engage in a neat way with the local church as the seed is sown, then join a nurture group, then share in growth. The vital thing is that all three core disciplines are practised in an ongoing way, owned by the Church and undergirded with prayer.

Learning the Faith

Different patterns of catechesis are based around different educational methodology. It is important for the group leaders to know that the authors have tried to work with an explicit but evolving methodology which we believe is helpful and appropriate for the times in which we live and faithful to the broader Christian and specifically Anglican tradition in which we are working.

We have a working list of seven basic principles.

1 God reveals himself gradually to those who follow him and God's call comes in different ways to different people.

The divine plan of Revelation is realized simultaneously by deeds and words which are intrinsically bound up with each other and shed light on each other. It involves a specific, divine pedagogy. God communicates himself to man gradually. He prepares him to welcome by stages the supernatural Revelation that is to culminate in the person and mission of the incarnate Word, Jesus Christ.

CATECHISM OF THE CATHOLIC CHURCH

God's great plan of revelation unfolds gradually in the Scriptures and culminates in God's revelation of himself in Jesus Christ. In the same way, in many individual encounters within the Scriptures we see God revealing himself step by step to those who would follow him.

The journey of the disciples in the gospels is one of gradual discovery and of seeing who Jesus is. On the Road to Emmaus we witness Jesus revealing himself to the two disciples who walk with him gradually through listening and loving attention, through Scripture and finally in the breaking of the bread (Luke 24). In the Acts of the Apostles, we share in Peter's ongoing discovery of the cosmic significance of Christ as he is led to understand what God is doing even among the Gentiles (Acts 10).

We also see in the Scriptures the ways in which God deals with different people. Some are called who are willing to serve and surrender themselves, like the prophet Isaiah who declares: 'Here I am; send me!' (Isaiah 6.8). Others are called who are reluctant to different ministries and aware of their own inadequacies.

There are moments of clarity and encounter with God in most journeys to Christian faith. These are always part of a longer process or journey. Sometimes they are in continuity with what has gone before. At other times there is a discontinuity and a sudden turning around (as in Saul's conversion on the Road to Damascus – Acts 9).

Those who work with people first coming to faith need to be alert to these different ways in which God works in human lives and to be open to the many different ways in which people experience the grace of God. Catechesis forms a living community where people are enabled to share this experience with others and so understand it more fully.

2 To become a Christian is to encounter the risen Christ in the Scriptures, in Christian community, in personal prayers and in the Eucharist. That encounter is life changing.

The roads people follow to faith are different but the end point is the same. The goal of all Christian catechesis is to enable men and women to encounter the risen Christ, to place their faith in him, to receive salvation and to follow Jesus Christ as his disciples.

This encounter with the risen Christ happens in many different ways but four means of grace in particular are identified in the Scriptures and remain vital in the life of the Church.

Those who became Christians on the day of Pentecost 'devoted themselves to the apostles teaching and fellowship, to the breaking of bread and the prayers' (Acts 2.42).

Catechesis must take seriously this need to encounter the risen Christ through these four means of grace especially, and so be founded on Scripture, intentionally nurture Christian community, draw people into participation in the Eucharist and be set in the context of living prayer.

Those who lead groups for catechesis need to be prepared to share something of themselves and also be prepared to grow small Christian communities as a key focus of their work.

3 Growing in Christian faith is therefore not simply about growth in understanding but is growth in character, in relationship, in response to God's grace, and in community.

According to Jesus, the kingdom of God is like a mustard seed 'which, when it is sown upon the ground, is the smallest of all the seeds of the earth. [32]Yet when it is sown it grows up and becomes the greatest of all shrubs, and puts forth large branches, so that the birds of the air can make nests in its shade' (Mark 4.31–32).

Transformation happens in a variety of ways as a person comes to know Christ. However, it will not only be a transformation of understanding. There may be specific sins from the past to be confessed and forgiven as part of coming to faith. Aspects of a person's lifestyle may need to be set right. Relationships may need to be healed and set right and forgiveness extended for past hurts. Order may need to be brought to chaotic lives.

These things will not happen in a moment. Growth in grace is the work of a lifetime. However, those who are involved in catechesis will need to help those preparing for baptism and confirmation to discern God's grace in their lives and to grow in these ways as they explore the Way.

4 The way in which we begin to learn about the Christian faith will condition and affect the way in which we continue to learn and grow in faith.

In any learning experience, we learn more through the informal or hidden curriculum than through the formal learning.

A group formed for catechesis will therefore communicate important lessons to those who come about the Christian life which are nothing to do with what is on the printed page of the material. These lessons will be contained in the culture and the atmosphere set by the group leaders.

Is every person's contribution welcomed? Is prayer taken seriously? Is there a genuine interest in everyone? Is the group pitched at a very intellectual level? Is there a practical application to what is being learned?

Those leading this work of catechesis need to be aware of this responsibility and provide the best environment they can for laying the foundations of discipleship.

5 The Holy Spirit is at work in the task of catechesis, through the common life of the group, through the Scriptures, the living word of God, and in the lives of individual group members.

One of the striking lessons of the New Testament is that neither Jesus himself nor Paul spend more than a few years with any group of disciples. Although learning and discipleship is a lifetime's task, initial formation and catechesis never seem to take longer than two or three years.

The reason for this is twofold. The first and most important is that God gives the Holy Spirit to every member of the Body of Christ. The Spirit's role is to dwell within the believer, to equip them for ministry and to 'teach you everything and remind you of all that I have said to you' (John 14.26).

The second reason is that the purpose of catechesis is not to create disciples who are dependent on those who teach them but disciples who are mature enough to take their place in the Body of Christ and in the world, and exercise gifts and ministries, including leading others to faith.

It is vital therefore that all those involved in catechesis are focused on the end goal of creating mature, interdependent groups of disciples rather than Christians who are forever pastorally dependent on others. It is also vital that all new Christians are introduced to and experience the life and work of the Holy Spirit following the pattern of the apostles (Acts 2.38, 8.14–16, 18.26–27 and 19.1–7).

6 To be a disciple is to be a lifelong learner of truths about the faith. Catechesis should therefore prepare the group for this lifetime of discipleship.

Again the Scriptures bear witness to the call to every Christian to continue to learn and to grow in wisdom through the whole of life.

Catechesis must avoid the sense that a period of instruction about the Christian life leads then to a later period when there is no need to go on learning and growing. There is always more to know of God and to learn about the Christian way. The circumstances and cycle of our lives mean that the gospel will mean different things in early life, in middle years and in old age. There is a need to continue growing continuously in our discipleship.

Catechesis must therefore point beyond itself to the lifelong commitment to learning and to grow as a disciple.

7 God's call is to know God as Father, Son and Holy Spirit and to enjoy God for ever. However, God's call is also to a lifetime of offering ourselves in Christian discipleship. Catechesis is about helping a new Christian recognize and receive God's grace and gifts and to begin to exercise their gifts in ministry and explore their vocation.

Growth in understanding as a Christian must embrace the call to whole life discipleship; the call to offer our best gifts to God and our time and resources in God's service.

As Paul writes in Romans:

> I appeal to you therefore, brothers and sisters, by the mercies of God, to present your bodies as a living sacrifice, holy and acceptable to God, which is your spiritual worship. [2]Do not be conformed to this world but be transformed by the renewing of your minds, so that you may discern what is the will of God – what is good and acceptable and perfect.
>
> ROMANS 12.1–2

pilgrim

Gathering a Group Together

How then should you begin to draw a small group of people together to be part of a *Pilgrim* group?

You will need to plan four or five months in advance. Don't wait until you have five expressions of interest from enquirers and then arrange the group. Plan in faith that as you are praying and sowing the seed of the gospel, so there will be some kind of harvest of people who want to find out more. And aim for this to happen on an annual basis.

Putting on a *Pilgrim* group can become a normal part of the annual cycle of parish life as you weave the work of evangelism, catechesis and discipleship into the fabric of church ministry. So put the dates in the church diary in advance and sort out the practical questions of when and where you will meet. Make sure the venue and time are suitable for those whom you envisage might come.

Also decide in advance who the leaders of the group will be. Ideally you need at least two people and, if possible, three. Their commitment is to work with the group through the first stage of the material. They will between them help gather the group together, lead the sessions, and, most importantly of all, help the group to become a community. To do this they will need to be committed to the group for up to a year. Perhaps one or more leaders might want to journey beyond that as the group enters the second stage of *Pilgrim*, focusing on discipleship.

Those leading the group will offer different gifts, but at least one should have the skills to facilitate a small group learning together and to guide the agenda of each evening. This normally means some theological training, so it is helpful if your team of leaders includes someone who is ordained or a Reader or Licensed Lay Minister or Evangelist, or someone who has experience and training for this sort of ministry. But not all the leaders need these gifts.

The leaders should have time to get to know the group members and to help them grow in their own faith and discipleship. Sharing in leading a group of this kind is a great privilege and it's not usually hard to recruit people for the role. Also there may be someone in the church who has the potential for this ministry and who needs to learn on the job as an apprentice.

The nature and purpose of the group needs to be communicated to the whole church. If the whole community understands what this group is for then they are more likely to have the confidence to suggest it to family and friends or to come themselves. Here is a sample description you could use on your church website or in your weekly news-sheet.

Pilgrim

Once a year St Agatha's offers a group for enquirers and new Christians who want to learn more about the Christian faith.

This year the group will meet on Thursday evenings in the Church Lounge at 7.30 pm starting on 1 November. The initial commitment is for six weeks but we hope to go on meeting through to May next year.

The group is for:

● those who have recently started coming to Church

● those who want the chance to think about Christian faith

● those preparing for baptism or confirmation

● those who have been Christians for many years and want to visit the roots of their faith again.

This year the *Pilgrim* group will be led by Dave Jones, Miranda Smith and Mike Smith. For more information contact the number or email below or speak to us after Church.

Please pass on news about the group to anyone you know who may be interested.

You will want to spread the net wide and make the group as well known as you can through posters and the church news-sheet and some simple printed invitations.

Most people will come only if the publicity material is backed up with a conversation and a personal invitation from the person who knows them best already in the life of the church, perhaps supported by a conversation with the group leaders.

How the conversation goes will of course depend on the two people involved. It may be helpful to emphasize:

- that no commitment to Christian faith or knowledge of faith is involved at the beginning
- there are lots of opportunities to ask questions
- everyone will be in the same boat
- it's a good chance to get to know people
- everyone at some point in their lives would benefit from exploring the Christian faith in this kind of way
- no one will be put on the spot
- most people find this kind of group really enjoyable.

You may want to include a meal as part of the evening, depending on the setting and the resources you have available. But whatever you do, hospitality will be a key ingredient, and someone needs to be responsible for organizing refreshments of some sort at each session.

Sometimes it can be helpful if an enquirer comes with someone who is already a Christian and member of the church. Some churches formalize this and call these people 'sponsors'. But it is best not to have a hard and fast rule about it. This is a detail to be worked out locally.

There may be some practical questions to address, such as offers of help with babysitting or lifts to and from the group meetings.

People learn in different ways. For that reason it's always helpful to have a resource box of short books and DVDs of talks; Christian music on CD; and details of other events taking place which the group may find useful as the course moves forward. Short promotional films and other resources to help you in publicising the course will be available via www.pilgrimcourse.org to help you attract interest online as well as in print.

The most important preparation is prayer. Paul writes in 1 Corinthians 3.6 : 'I planted, Apollos watered, but God gave the growth.' This informal gathering of a handful of people is providing an opportunity and place where men and women can encounter the truth of the gospel and the power of the living God.

Make sure that others in the life of the church are praying for the group and for its leaders both as you gather people together and as the group begins to meet. Experience suggests that in this kind of ministry it is wise to expect setbacks of different kinds. There may often be a sense of spiritual conflict and struggle as you seek to provide this safe and secure environment to learn about the Christian faith and to build community. When that happens, keep praying and keep going. It's often a sign that you are on exactly the right track.

Leading the Sessions

The *Pilgrim* material is designed to be flexible and adaptable. This includes the time you take for each session. We think the material will fit into an hour, but in preparing the material we've had a 75–90-minute session in mind, so you may need to do some pruning if you decide an hour is better for your context. Don't feel you have to do everything.

Each leader needs a copy of this leader's guide; and each group member a copy of the member's booklet for the course. People don't need to read it beforehand, though bear in mind quite a few will. Once they have the book, it is inevitable that they will look ahead. In some groups there may be people who are uncomfortable with written material. Bear this in mind. In some cases you may decide to dispense with the booklet altogether and just use it as your guide. But these cases will be rare.

A short film for each session is on the *Pilgrim* website. You don't have to use films, but they are a very helpful way of introducing the theme of each session. You can play the films directly from the website on a laptop and projector, or transfer them in advance to a DVD and show them on a television with a DVD player or computer.

The first time you use the material you'll need at least one planning meeting for the leaders to plan the sessions themselves (as well as the initial planning meeting that was about drawing the group together). You may want to briefly review each session between meetings and reflect on what has worked well and what hasn't.

Each session of the course follows a similar pattern.

Refreshments as people arrive can be very helpful in settling the group.

Each session has a clearly stated **theme and purpose** that is given at the beginning of the group member's material. After an initial **welcome**, begin by briefly introducing the theme of the session. At the first meeting of the group it is important to give members a chance to introduce themselves (perhaps by talking to the person next to them and introducing them to the whole group). It is also important for the leaders to say a bit more about themselves and the purpose of the course.

Some basic **ground rules** can help such as asking people to come on time for meetings; to send apologies if they can't come; to be courteous if there is disagreement with someone; and to encourage people to ask questions honestly and openly.

Each session begins with **short prayers** in the form of a simple liturgy set out in the member's booklet. One of the group leaders should lead this at the beginning but you may want to involve the group members as you go through the course. People will arrive with many different things on their minds and it is important to provide a space for them to settle and to focus in this time set aside on following Jesus Christ. Each member of the group will be at a different place on the journey towards faith. Be sensitive to this. But gently leading people into prayer is one of the best ways of helping them to know God.

Therefore do not skip this part of the session, even if the group is made up of enquirers who are not even sure that they believe in God. A liturgical order for prayer helps here and enables participation much more easily than simply a time of open prayer (though this can form part of the prayer time).

This is also your opportunity to introduce group members to different styles of prayer, and to encourage them to build times of prayer into daily life.

With the welcome the prayers should take about ten minutes.

There then follows a brief section headed **conversation** in the member's booklet. This is just an icebreaker question to get people thinking and talking. It should only take a few minutes as people buzz and share with each other. It is not intended to be a *long* conversation!

The conversation should last about five minutes.

After this the **film** can be shown. It can be downloaded from www. pilgrimcourse.org. The film aims to inspire the group to start thinking about the theme and purpose of the session. All you need to do is encourage response. There doesn't need to be discussion at this point unless it arises naturally.

Each film is about three or four minutes long.

The film is followed by a **reflection on Scripture**. There is a Bible passage for each session and over the whole course a breadth and variety of Scripture will be looked at.

The reflective and critical reading of Scripture is a central feature of *Pilgrim*. Our approach to Christian nurture and formation is rooted in Scripture. Together the group learns to read, digest and reflect on it in ways that will be helpful for the living out of the faith each day as well as understanding what it means. The leader therefore needs to be prepared by having looked at and thought about the passage before the session. The leader is not required to tell the group what the passage means, but to draw out their own responses and questions and then respond to them. There will, of course, be times when explanation is required. Sometimes a guide to this is given in the 'essay' that follows. Sometimes the leader will need to provide this. But there are simple explanatory notes on each of the biblical passages in the member's handbook.

By following a similar pattern in each session we hope that when the first stage of the course is completed the group will not necessarily need a leader at all, but will be able to run itself.

This is the pattern for reading Scripture that we ask you to follow in each session. It is based on the ancient monastic way of reading Scripture known as *Lectio Divina* (which simply means godly reading).

- Read the Bible passage through once aloud.

- Invite people to think about it in silence.

- Read the passage again – perhaps asking someone else to read, or divide the passage between different voices. This will depend a bit on the group.

- Invite people to say out loud a word or a phrase from the passage that has struck them. At the beginning make it clear that it's fine to pass and not say anything.

- After a few moments of quiet, read the passage a third time.

- Either in the whole group, or with their neighbour in twos or threes, invite people to share with each other why this word or phrase jumped out at them, what it might mean and what questions it raises.

- Respond as appropriate.

Reflecting on the Scriptures together should take about thirty minutes.

The main teaching content of the session follows. At its heart, each session has a short reflective article. These articles are written by a range of different people: bishops, prominent theologians and church leaders, men and women. Together these reflections form a resource for sharing and reflecting on the Christian faith.

The article is in the booklet and on the website as a sound file from www.pilgrimcourse.org. Although the article is not an actual commentary on the Bible passage you have just looked at, it flows from it and helps develop the main theme of the session.

Either read the article aloud, invite people to read it in silence, or listen to it.

In the middle and/or at the end of each article there are questions for discussion. The questions are designed to help the group think creatively about the theme of the session. Make sure you have looked at them in advance and started to think about them before the session begins. Although you are not expected to have all the answers, it is important to have begun thinking about how the session will proceed, and what might come up. By all means add or substitute questions of your own if you think they will work better for your group. Encourage the group to respond in the way that is right for them.

A key part of learning about the Christian faith in this kind of group is the opportunity for group members to ask the questions that are central to their search and journey. After you have looked at the reflection and the questions, we suggest one of the leaders draws this part of the session to a close with a short summary of the theme and then invites questions from the group on this topic or any others they are encountering.

Reading/listening to the article and the discussion should take about thirty minutes.

The session concludes with **prayer**. This time a short set prayer and also an opportunity for one of the leaders to gather together in prayer the things that have been said and explored in the session.

This emphasis on prayer and reflection in *Pilgrim* is our of recognition that one of the best ways to introduce people to the Christian faith is to provide a place where they feel at ease and can freely ask questions, and where they learn to read the Bible and to pray.

In the final session of each course a slightly longer time of prayer is appropriate. This provides a moment to review the short course, give thanks for what has been learned and also an opportunity for a response of faith and personal commitment.

The final prayers should be no more than five minutes.

The session concludes with a short challenge to live and reflect on what has been explored. Sometimes group members are asked or encouraged to do something practical.

And at the end of each session are a number of quotations from Christian writers and theologians down through the centuries and to the present day. These short readings are included to help demonstrate our participation in a long and unfolding tradition of reading Scripture and pondering the meaning and impact of Jesus Christ, and to enable the group member to go a little deeper into the theme of the session. Encourage people to look at the passages in the coming week.

The final sending out should be no more than five minutes.

With refreshments at the beginning and/or the end the whole session should last about an hour and three-quarters that is a 9.15 pm finish for a session starting at 7.30 pm.

Caring for the people in the group

Some people will come on this course because they want to find out about the Christian faith. They won't necessarily be attending church services at all. Others will come for a kind of refresher course. They will be church goers, but won't necessarily know a lot about their faith. Others will be fringe people, who come to church occasionally.

Becoming a Christian is like a journey. As you lead this group you need to be sensitive to the fact that in each group there will be people at different stages of this journey. Your job is to lead them. In this respect you are their pastor as much as their teacher.

When a group meets for the first time it is important that people are given time to introduce and get to know each other. You also need to be ready to depart from the pattern of the session and be led by the questions and concerns of the group. But you mustn't let any one person's agenda dominate.

Remember that as each session begins, people arrive from busy and often pressured lives and will be carrying some of those concerns with them. This is why refreshments and prayer at the beginning of the session can help. It enables people to wind down and get ready for the session and also share with each other. Our aim is that this little group becomes, in its own distinctive way, a cell or community of the church, enabled, if appropriate, to go on meeting, learning, praying, serving and supporting each other even after the course has finished.

As you get to know the individuals, try to ensure that each voice is heard and that everyone has the opportunity to speak if they want to. Though bear in mind, being silent doesn't necessarily mean not participating!

Occasionally, someone will talk too much. Have a quiet word with them after a session rather than embarrassing them during it.

Difficult questions will arise. Both tough theological questions and, as the group grows in mutual trust, hard personal matters. If you cannot answer or address the difficult theological questions, be honest about it; make a note of the questions and endeavour to find out for a following session. With personal matters it will sometimes be necessary to see and care for individuals outside the session itself, though the group itself can often be a place where sharing and mutual listening can bring healing solace, and then be offered to God in prayer.

Occasionally people may decide that the group is not for them (which is absolutely fine). Try and make a good ending to their time and leave the door open for people to pick up another group at a future date.

The initial commitment of the group is for six weeks but with a possibility of the group continuing. By at least four weeks in you need to make plans for the next part of the group's life and encourage people to take part. You need to decide as a group of leaders whether to welcome anyone else who wants to join at that point.

You will find that the group has its own life and dynamic as people meet together regularly. The initial group will not know one another. You may want to focus on questions and exercises that help people to tell their story easily. People normally make an effort to be polite but there can be some awkward silences.

As the group get to know one another better, there will be more to talk about but you may also find people are more honest with one another. Do your best to help the group through conflict and disagreement so they come to appreciate one another.

At that point it can help the life of the group to have a common task such as arranging a meal together or undertaking a simple act of service (such as making the coffee after church on Sunday).

Remember that it does take time for a group of people to form and get to know one another – and normally longer than the initial six-week course.

It may be helpful as the group develops for the leaders to meet occasionally with individual group members outside the group meetings to reflect on how things are going. Not everyone feels able to share or ask questions in a group setting.

Above all, be sensitive to what God is doing in the life of the group and in the life of its members. You will often be surprised and have the sense that you are treading on holy ground here and individuals encounter the love of Christ and the power of the Holy Spirit and their lives are transformed.

Looking after the practicalities

Welcome. Welcome. Welcome.

The invitation to know Christ is also an invitation to be part of his body, the Church, therefore hospitality, welcome and sensitivity to the needs of different individuals is central to the whole process of initiation. The truth of our words will be measured by our actions.

So make sure you have a good room to meet in. *Pilgrim* groups will probably meet in people's homes, though it could be in a church hall, a café or a pub.

Make sure there are refreshments. What is appropriate will vary from group to group, place to place and session to session. But make sure something is prepared each time. You may decide to have a meal together. There should always be drinks available, either at the beginning or end of the session – or both.

Keep to time. Encourage people to arrive on time. Make sure you finish on time. If some people want to stay on chatting for longer, then this is fine so long as it is okay with the host. But make it clear that others can go if they need to.

pilgrim

PART FOUR:
PILGRIM RESOURCES

Pilgrim Books and Website

The *Pilgrim* programme consists of two stages.

Follow Stage

There are four courses in this first Follow Stage of the *Pilgrim* programme. The Follow Stage is designed for new enquirers and for those who are very new to faith. Each of these courses consists of six weekly sessions:

● *Turning to Christ* (published Oct. 2013)

● *The Lord's Prayer* (published Oct. 2013)

● *The Commandments* (published Jan. 2014)

● *The Beatitudes* (published Jan. 2014)

The four courses in the Follow Stage are accompanied by this *Leader's Guide*, designed to assist those leading groups through the Follow Stage.

Grow Stage

The second half the *Pilgrim* programme is known as the Grow Stage, because it aims to help readers go further into discipleship and learn more. Like the Follow Stage, the Grow Stage also consists of four courses:

● *The Creeds* (published Sept. 2014)

● *The Eucharist* (published Sept. 2014)

● *The Bible* (published Jan. 2015)

● *Church and Kingdom* (published Jan. 2015)

A Grow Stage *Leader's Guide* is also published in September 2014.

Formats

All titles published as part of the *Pilgrim* programme are available in print and in e-book formats. Please visit the *Pilgrim* website for more details.

Website

The dedicated *Pilgrim* website address is www.pilgrimcourse.org. Helpful resources to support those using the course can be found here, including audio recordings of the Reflections included in each session, short videos to introduce the sessions and other support materials.

Please visit the website regularly for details of brand new supporting materials, information, updates, and to contribute any comments you would like to make. You can also go to the website to register your e-mail address for e-alerts.

Twitter

Twitter: @pilgrimcourse

Liturgical Resources

You will want to pay careful attention to how the group is connected to the wider congregations (or group of congregations) you are part of. This is a two-way process.

It is helpful to make sure that the group is mentioned in the Sunday intercessions as it begins to meet and at key points in its life and not just in the notices.

Once the group has become established you will be able to gain a sense of who may be preparing for baptism or confirmation, or the renewal of baptismal vows. It will be helpful to identify an occasion when this liturgical celebration can happen. For candidates who are being confirmed it may not be possible for the service to be in your own parish church each year.

For this reason it can be very helpful to celebrate three points in the journey of the group as part of a Sunday service when the community gathers. The Church of England has an authorized liturgy to support the work of catechesis and to support disciples in the way of Christ. This material is contained in the sections 'Rites Supporting Disciples on the Way of Christ' and 'Rites of Affirmation: Approaching Baptism' in *Common Worship: Christian Initiation* (Church House Publishing, 2006).

Welcome of disciples on the Way of Faith

The first point in the group's journey would be at the end of the first Follow course as enquirers commit themselves to go on in their journey of exploration. If you are following the timetable outlined above, this service would take place either in Advent, as the group concludes its final session before Christmas, or in the New Year as it gathers again for the second short course, ideally on the first Sunday of Epiphany as the Church celebrates the Baptism of Christ.

This short rite makes provision for sponsors to support the candidates. These would be Christian friends who agree to pray for and meet regularly with the candidates, to welcome them into the life of the congregation and support them in the Way.

Welcome of Disciples on The Way of Faith

Notes

1 This rite is intended for those who, after an initial exploration of the Christian faith, wish to learn the Christian Way within the life of the people of God. It is not intended for initial enquirers, but for those who want to commit themselves to continuing the journey of faith. One or more members of the Church should be invited to be the companion(s) of each new disciple, and to act as their sponsors. Those sponsors may be commissioned during this rite.

2 The Welcome should be included in an act of public worship, and may be used before the collect, after the sermon or before the peace. The rite might begin outside the church building or at the church door, where the new disciples are welcomed by the Christian community, and particularly by their sponsors, and accompanied into the church in procession.

3 It may be appropriate to give the new disciple a gift to express the welcome and support of the church community.

Welcome

The minister may introduce the Welcome in these or similar words

Today it is our joy and privilege to welcome *N and N* as *disciples* on the Way of Christ. *They* are among us as a sign of the journey of faith to which we are all called.

The minister invites the disciples to stand before the people with their sponsors. The sponsors introduce them, and the minister says

We thank God for his presence in your *lives*
and for the grace that has brought you here today.

We welcome you.
What is it that you seek?

The disciples may reply in their own words, or may say

To learn the Way of Christ.

The minister addresses the congregation

We welcome *N and N*
in the love and hope of Christ.
Will you support and pray for *them*,
and learn with *them* the Way of Christ?
All **With the help of God, we will.**

The minister may introduce the sponsors and address them using these or other suitable words

Will you accompany *N and N* on the journey of faith,
supporting *them* with friendship, love and prayer?
With the help of God, we will.

The minister may commission the sponsors using these or other suitable words

May God give you the gift of love
to serve *N and N* whom he loved first.
May God give you the gift of faith
to share the good news of his kingdom.
May God give you the gift of joy
as you journey together with Jesus our Lord.
And may the blessing of God almighty,
the Father, the Son and the Holy Spirit,
be among you and remain with you always. Amen.

The minister then addresses each candidate separately or the group together

Will you receive the sign of the cross,
as a mark of Christ's love for you as you explore his Way?
I will.

*The minister makes the sign of the cross on the forehead of each candidate.
The sponsors may be invited to sign the candidates with the cross. The
minister says*

Receive the sign of the cross.
May Christ our Redeemer,
who claims you for his own,
deliver you from evil and guide you on the Way.

Where a candidate is already baptized, the minister uses these words

Receive the sign of the cross.
May Christ our Redeemer,
who in your baptism claimed you for his own,
protect and guide you.

*Prayer may be offered for each new disciple. After all have been prayed
with, the minister says this or a similar prayer. It may be said over each
disciple or the whole group.*

God of life,
you give us the gift of faith.
Guide *N and N* by your wisdom
and surround *them* with your love.
Deepen *their* knowledge of Christ
and set *their* feet on the Way that leads to life.
May your people uphold *them* in love,
find in *them* a sign of hope,
and learn with *them* the Way of Christ.
All **Amen.**

*A gift expressing welcome to the new disciple from the congregation may
be given.*

Call and Celebration of the Decision to be Baptized or Confirmed or to Affirm Baptismal Faith

The second point in the group's journey is the rite in which people acknowledge their commitment to Jesus Christ and their intention to be baptized or confirmed or to renew their baptismal vows. This enables those who are being enrolled as candidates to be introduced to the congregation in a simple way so that the congregation can pray for them and encourage them on the journey. If you are following the timetable outlined above, the first Sunday in Lent is a good moment for this to be part of the liturgy.

Call and Celebration of the Decision to be Baptized or Confirmed or to Affirm Baptismal Faith

Notes

1 The Call is intended for those who wish to continue on the Way, following a period of exploration and regular involvement in the Christian community.

2 The Call should be included in an act of public worship, and may be used before the collect, after the sermon or before the peace.

3 At the Signing with the Cross, a priest may anoint the candidate with pure olive oil, reflecting the practice of athletes preparing for a contest. It is appropriate that the oil should be that consecrated by the bishop for Signing with the Cross. If oil is used, care should be taken that the candidates understand the symbolism and significance of anointing. When a candidate for baptism is anointed during the Call, oil is not used for the Signing with the Cross in Baptism; however, oil mixed with fragrant spices (traditionally called chrism), expressing the blessings of the messianic era and the richness of the Holy Spirit, is used to accompany the prayer after the baptism, if it is not to be used at Confirmation.

4 Where a disciple has already been baptized, the second form is used at the Signing with the Cross.

Call and Celebration

The minister may introduce the Call in these or similar words

Today it is our joy and privilege to welcome *N and N*,
disciples with us on the Way of Christ.
They are among us as a sign of the journey of faith to which we are all
called.

*The minister invites the disciples to stand before the people with their
sponsors. The disciples are presented to the congregation by their
sponsors, and some words of personal commendation may be said. The
minister says*

We thank God for his presence in your *lives*
and for the grace that has brought you here today.
What is it that you seek?

The disciples may reply in their own words, or may say

To follow the Way of Christ.

*The minister may ask the sponsors to confirm the candidates' commitment
to worship, prayer and the fellowship of the Church, and their readiness
to study and to understand their story as part of the people of God. The
names of those who seek initiation may be added to a book dedicated for
that purpose.*

*The minister then addresses each candidate separately or the group
together*

Will you receive the sign of the cross
as a mark of Christ's love for you
as you explore his Way?
I will.

*The minister makes the sign of the cross on the forehead of each candidate.
The sponsors may be invited to sign the candidates with the cross. The
minister says*

Receive the sign of the cross.
May Christ our Redeemer,
who claims you for his own,
deliver you from evil and guide you on the Way.

Where a candidate is already baptized, the minister uses these words

Receive the sign of the cross.
May Christ our Redeemer,
who in your baptism claimed you for his own,
protect and guide you.

A copy of a Gospel is presented, with these words

Receive this book.
It is the good news of God's love.
Take it as your guide.

The candidates remain in front of the congregation for the prayers of intercession. This or other similar forms may be used.

N and N, who *are our brothers and sisters, have* already travelled a long road. We rejoice with *them* in the gentle guidance of God. Let us pray that *they* may press onwards, until *they come* to share fully in the Way of Christ.

May God the Father reveal his Christ to *them* more and more
with every passing day.
Lord, in your mercy
All **hear our prayer.**

May *they* undertake with generous *hearts* and *souls* whatever God
may ask of *them.*
Lord, in your mercy
All **hear our prayer.**

May *they* have our sincere and unfailing support every step
of the way.
Lord, in your mercy
All **hear our prayer.**

May *their hearts* and ours become more responsive to the needs
of others.
Lord, in your mercy
All **hear our prayer.**

In due time may *they* come *to baptism / to confirmation / to reaffirm
their baptismal faith,* and receive the renewal of the Holy Spirit.
Lord, in your mercy
All **hear our prayer.**

Celebration after an Initiation Service outside the Parish

The final point in the group's journey would be a suitable Sunday
shortly after the Baptism and Confirmation service when the whole
congregation is gathered and the newly baptized and confirmed (and
those who have renewed their vows) are welcomed formally by God's
people and prayed for by their own congregation and community. Where
the Baptism and Confirmation was in the candidates' own parish there
would be no call for this service.

It may also be helpful to include in this service the Affirmation of the
Christian Way, which is reproduced separately below but which should
be incorporated before the final blessing.

Celebration after an Initiation Service Outside the Parish

Note

When baptism, confirmation and/or affirmation of baptismal faith have been celebrated
outside the parish, for example in the cathedral church or in another church within
the deanery, it may be appropriate for the regular congregation to acknowledge this

important transition. If this Celebration is used, it should normally be included in the principal service on the following Sunday.

Pastoral Introduction

This may be read by those present before the service begins.

Baptism marks the beginning of a journey with God which continues for the rest of our lives. In the last *months N and N* have been exploring the meaning of baptism in Jesus Christ. They have looked together at the call to discipleship in the world and in the Church. They have sought to understand the responsibilities of discipleship in today's world. We celebrate with them their baptism / confirmation by Bishop *N* / affirmation of baptismal faith and will seek to learn with them the Way of Christ.

Prayers of Intercession

At the Prayers of Intercession the following may be used

We pray for *N and N*,
that they may continue to grow in the grace of Christ,
take their place among the company of your people,
and reflect your glory in the world.
Lord, in your mercy
All **hear our prayer.**

The Welcome and Peace

The president says

I present to you *N and N* who have recently been baptized / confirmed / affirmed their baptismal faith. Will you welcome them and uphold them in their new life in Christ?
All **With the help of God, we will.**

There is one Lord, one faith, one baptism:
N and N, by one Spirit we are all baptized into one body.
All **We welcome you into the fellowship of faith;**
we are children of the same heavenly Father;
we welcome you.

An opportunity may be given for testimony.
The president introduces the Peace in these or other suitable words

We are all one in Christ Jesus.
We belong to him through faith,
heirs of the promise of the Spirit of peace.
The peace of the Lord be always with you
All **and also with you.**

A minister may say

Let us offer one another a sign of peace.

All may exchange a sign of peace.

Affirmation of the Christian Way

Note

This may be used in public worship when special significance is being given to the presence of disciples on the Way, for example at the Welcome or the Call. It may also be suitable in informal settings as an introduction or reminder about the shape of the Way. Where appropriate, it may be led by two or three people.

Affirmation of the Christian Way

As we follow the Way of Christ,
we affirm the presence of God among us,
Father, Son and Holy Spirit.

God calls us to share in worship.
Jesus said, where two or three are gathered in my name,
I am there among them.
All **Jesus, you are the Way: guide us on our journey.**

God calls us to share in prayer.
Jesus said, remain in me, and I will remain in you.
All **Jesus, you are the Way: guide us on our journey.**

God calls us to share the Scriptures.
Jesus met his disciples on the road
and opened the Scriptures to them.
All **Jesus, you are the Way: guide us on our journey.**

God calls us to share in communion.
Jesus said, do this in remembrance of me.
All **Jesus, you are the Way: guide us on our journey.**

God calls us to share in service.
Jesus said, as you do it for the least of these, you do it for me.
All **Jesus, you are the Way: guide us on our journey.**

God calls us to share the good news.
Jesus said, go and make disciples of all nations.
All **Jesus, you are the Way: guide us on our journey.**

The Presentation of the Four Texts

The Church of England's liturgy recognizes the importance of the Four Texts which are at the heart of *Pilgrim*. Separate short services are offered in *Common Worship: Initiation Services* to mark the handing over of the Four Texts in public worship.

These can be used in the main Sunday service or in the final session of each of the four Follow courses.

Other Books and Resources

Leading small groups

Many group leaders will be expert at leading small groups and need no further help, but if you do not feel confident about how to lead a small group effectively you may find the following books helpful.

Arnold, Jeffrey, *The Big Book on Small Groups*, revised, Inter Varsity Press Connect, 2009.
Mcbride, N. F., *How to Lead Small Groups*, NavPress, 1990.
Morris, Karen, and Rod Morris, *Leading Better Bible Studies: Essential Skills for Effective Small Groups*, Aquila Press, 1997.
Rogers, Jenny, *Adults Learning*, 5th edn, Open University Press, 2007.

Discovering more about faith

There may be people in your group who want to read more about the Christian faith. These are good 'beginner level' books.

Bell, Rob, *What We Talk About When We Talk About God*, Collins, 2013.
Lewis, C. S., *Mere Christianity*, Collins, 2012.
Polkinghorne, John, *Belief in God in an Age of Science*, Yale, 2003.
Radcliffe, Timothy, *What is the Point of Being a Christian*, Continuum/ Burns & Oates, 2005.
Spufford, Francis, *Unapologetic: Why, Despite Everything, Christianity Can Still Make Surprising Emotional Sense*, Faber & Faber, 2013.
Stott, John, *Basic Christianity*, new edn, Inter Varsity Press, 2008.
Ward, Keith, *Christianity: A Guide for the Perplexed*, reprint, SPCK Publishing, 2007.
Wright, Tom, *Simply Christian*, SPCK Publishing, 2011.
Wright, Tom, *Simply Jesus – Who He Was, What He Did, Why It Matters*, SPCK Publishing, 2011.
Young, John, *Teach Yourself Christianity*, Hodder and Stoughton, 2003.

These books are more in depth introductions to Christian Doctrine.

Bromiley, Geoffrey W., *Historical Theology: An Introduction*, T & T Clark, 1978.

Ford, David, *Theology: A Very Short Introduction*, new edn, Oxford Paperbacks, 2000.

Higton, Mike, *Christian Doctrine*, SCM Press, 2008.

McGrath, Alister E., *Christian Theology: An Introduction*, 4th edn, Wiley-Blackwell, 2006.

Migliore, Daniel L., *Faith Seeking Understanding*, 2nd edn, William B Eerdmans Publishing Co, 2004.

Discovering more about *Lectio Divina*

One of the main pillars of this course is *Lectio Divina* – some people may want to learn more about the principles that lie behind it.

Bianchi, Enzo, *Words of Spirituality: Exploring the Inner Life*, SPCK Publishing, 2012.

Foster, David, *Reading with God: Lectio Divina*, Continuum International Publishing Group Ltd., 2005.

Paintner, Christine Valters, *Lectio Divina – the Sacred Art*, SPCK Publishing, 2012.

Smith, Martin, *The Word is Very Near You: A Guide to Praying with Scripture*, Darton, Longman & Todd, 1989.

Helpful handbooks and introductions for new Christians

Cottrell, Stephen and Stephen Croft, *How to Live*, Church House Publishing, 2011.

Cottrell, Stephen, *How to Pray*, Church House Publishing, 2011.

Mayfield, Sue, *Exploring Prayer,* Lion, 2007.

Pritchard, John, *How to Pray*, SPCK Publishing, 2011.

Discovering more about Anglicanism

This course is very clearly an Anglican discipleship. For people who want to learn more about Anglicanism, the following books will be helpful.

Chapman, Mark, *Anglicanism: A Very Short Introduction*, Oxford University Press, 2006.
Podmore, Colin, *Aspects of Anglican Identity*, Church House Publishing, 2005.
Redfern, Alistair, *Being Anglican*, Darton, Longman and Todd, 2000.
Spencer, Stephen, *SCM Studyguide: Anglicanism*, SCM Press, 2010.
Wells, Samuel, *What Anglicans Believe: An Introduction*, Canterbury Press, 2011.

More detailed books on Baptism

Earey, Mark, *Connecting with Baptism: A Practical Guide to Christian Initiation Today*, edited by Mark Earey, Trevor Lloyd, and Ian Tarrant, Church House Publishing, 2007.
Radcliffe, Timothy, *Take the Plunge: Living Baptism and Confirmation*, Burns & Oates, 2012.
Whitehead, Nick and Hazel Whitehead, *Baptism Matters*, Church House Publishing, 2012.

More detailed books on the Lord's Prayer

Crossan, John Dominic, *The Greatest Prayer: Rediscovering the Revolutionary Message of the Lord's Prayer*, SPCK Publishing, 2011.
Kendall, R. T., *The Lord's Prayer*, Hodder & Stoughton, 2011.
Wright, Tom, *The Lord and His Prayer*, SPCK Publishing, 2012.

More detailed books on the Commandments

Chan, Yiu Sing Lucas, *The Ten Commandments and the Beatitudes: Biblical Studies and Ethics for Real Life*, Rowman & Littlefield Publishers, 2012.

John, J., *Ten*, 1st edn, David C Cook, 2009.

More detailed books on the Beatitudes

Bonhoeffer, Dietrich, *The Cost of Discipleship*, SCM Press, 1976.

Chan, Yiu Sing Lucas, *The Ten Commandments and the Beatitudes: Biblical Studies and Ethics for Real Life*, Rowman & Littlefield Publishers, 2012.

Croft, Steven, *Jesus People: What next for the Church*, Church House Publishing, 2009.

Yancey, Philip, *The Jesus I Never Knew*, new edn, Zondervan Publishing House, 2002.

The Revised Catechism

I. THE CALL OF GOD: THE CHRISTIAN ANSWER

1 *What is your Christian name?*
My name is ....

2 *Who gave you this name?*
My parents and godparents gave me this name at my Baptism.

3 *What did God do for you in your Baptism?*
In my Baptism God called me to himself, and I was made a member of Christ, the child of God, and an inheritor of the kingdom of heaven.

4 *What did your godparents promise for you at your Baptism?*
At my Baptism my godparents made three promises to God for me: first, that I would renounce the devil and fight against evil; secondly, that I would hold fast the Christian Faith and put my whole trust in Christ as Lord and Saviour; thirdly, that I would obediently keep God's holy will and commandments and serve him faithfully all the days of my life.

5 *Are you bound to do as they promised?*
Yes, certainly, and by God's help I will.

II. CHRISTIAN BELIEF

6 *Where do you find a summary of this Christian Faith which you are bound to believe and hold fast?*
I find a summary of the Christian Faith in the Apostles' Creed and in the Nicene Creed.

7   *Repeat the Apostles' Creed.*
    I believe in God the Father almighty,
    creator of heaven and earth.
    I believe in Jesus Christ, his only Son, our Lord,
    who was conceived by the Holy Spirit,
    born of the Virgin Mary,
    suffered under Pontius Pilate,
    was crucified, died, and was buried,
    he descended to the dead.
    On the third day he rose again;
    he ascended into heaven,
    he is seated at the right hand of the Father,
    and he will come to judge the living and the dead.
    I believe in the Holy Spirit,
    the holy catholic Church,
    the communion of saints,
    the forgiveness of sins,
    the resurrection of the body,
    and the life everlasting.
    Amen.

8   *What do you learn from the Creeds?*
    From the Creeds I learn to believe in one God, Father, Son and
    Holy Spirit, who is the creator and ruler of the universe, and has
    made all things for his glory.

9   *What does the Church teach about God the Father?*
    The Church teaches that God the Father made me and all
    humankind, and that in love he sent his Son to reconcile the world
    to himself.

10 *What does the Church teach about God the Son?*
    The Church teaches that, for our salvation, God the Son became
    man and died for our sins; that he was raised victorious over
    death and was exalted to the throne of God as our advocate and
    intercessor; and that he will come as our judge and saviour.

11   *What does the Church teach about God the Holy Spirit?*
The Church teaches that God the Holy Spirit inspires all that is good in humankind; that he came in his fullness at Pentecost to be the giver of life in the Church, and that he enables me to grow in likeness to Jesus Christ.

Thus I learn to believe in one God, Father, Son and Holy Spirit, and this Holy Trinity I praise and magnify saying:

Glory be to the Father, and to the Son, and to the Holy Spirit: as it was in the beginning, is now, and ever shall be, world without end. Amen.

III. THE CHURCH AND MINISTRY

12   *What is the Church?*
The Church is the family of God and the Body of Christ through which he continues his reconciling work among humankind. Its members on earth enter it by baptism and are one company with those who worship God in heaven.

13   *How is the Church described in the Creeds?*
The Church is described as One, Holy, Catholic, and Apostolic.

14   *What do you mean by these words?*
By these words I mean that:

- the Church is *One* because, in spite of its divisions, it is one family under one Father, whose purpose is to unite all people in Jesus Christ our Lord;

- the Church is *Holy* because it is set apart by God for himself, through the Holy Spirit;

- the Church is *Catholic* because it is universal, for all nations and for all time, holding the Christian Faith in its fullness;

- the Church is *Apostolic* because it is sent to preach the gospel to the whole world, and receives divine authority and teaching from Christ through his Apostles.

15 *What orders of ministers are there in the Church?*
There are these orders of ministers in the Church:

Bishops, Priests, and Deacons.

16 *What is the work of a Bishop?*
The work of a Bishop is to be a chief shepherd and a ruler in the Church; to guard the Faith; to ordain and confirm; and to be the chief minister of the Word and Sacraments in his diocese.

17 *What is the work of a Priest?*
The work of a Priest is to preach the word of God, to teach, and to baptize; to celebrate the Holy Communion; to pronounce absolution and blessing in God's name; and to care for the people entrusted by the Bishop to his or her charge.

18 *What is the work of a Deacon?*
The work of a Deacon is to help the Priest both in the conduct of worship and in the care of souls.

19 *What is the Church of England?*
The Church of England is the ancient Church of this land, catholic and reformed. It proclaims and holds fast the doctrine and ministry of the One, Holy, Catholic, and Apostolic Church.

20 *What is the Anglican Communion?*
The Anglican Communion is a family of Churches within the universal Church of Christ, maintaining apostolic doctrine and order and in full communion with one another and with the Sees of Canterbury and York.

IV. CHRISTIAN OBEDIENCE

21 *The third promise made at your Baptism binds you to keep God's commandments all the days of your life. Where has God made these commandments known?*
God has made his commandments known in the Scriptures of the Old and New Testaments, especially in the teaching and example of our Lord Jesus Christ.

22 *Repeat the Ten Commandments found in the law of Moses.*
1 I am the Lord your God who brought you out of the land of Egypt, out of the house of slavery. You shall have no other gods but me.

2 You shall not make for yourself any idol, nor the likeness of anything that is in heaven above, or in the earth beneath, or in the water under the earth. You shall not bow down to them or serve them.

3 You shall not dishonour the name of the Lord your God.

4 Remember the Sabbath day and keep it holy. Six days you shall labour and do all your work; but the seventh day is the Sabbath of the Lord your God.

5 Honour your father and your mother.

6 You shall not commit murder.

7 You shall not commit adultery.

8 You shall not steal.

9 You shall not bear false witness against your neighbour.

10 You shall not covet anything which belongs to your neighbour.

23   *Repeat the words of our Lord Jesus Christ about God's command-*
     ments.
     Our Lord Jesus Christ said:
     The first commandment is this:
     'Hear, O Israel, the Lord our God is the only Lord.
     You shall love the Lord your God with all your heart,
     with all your soul, with all your mind,
     and with all your strength.'

     The second is this: 'Love your neighbour as yourself.'
     There is no other commandment greater than these.
     On these two commandments hang all the law and the prophets.

24   *What then is your duty towards God?*
     My duty towards God is:

     1   to worship him as the only true God, to love, trust, and obey
         him, and by witness of my words and deeds to bring others
         to serve him;

     2   to allow no created thing to take his place, but to use my
         time, my gifts, and my possessions as one who must give
         an account to him;

     3   to reverence him in thought, word, and deed;

     4   to keep the Lord's day for worship, prayer, and rest from
         work.

25   *What is your duty towards your neighbour?*
     My duty towards my neighbour is:

     5   to love, respect, and help my parents; to honour the Queen;
         to obey those in authority over me in all things lawful and
         good; and to fulfil my duties as a citizen;

     6   to hurt nobody by word or deed; to bear no grudge or
         hatred in my heart; to promote peace among all people; to
         be courteous to all; and to be kind to all God's creatures;

7 to be clean in thought, word, and deed, controlling my bodily desires through the power of the Holy Spirit who dwells within me; and if called to the state of marriage to live faithfully in it;

8 to be honest and fair in all I do; not to steal or cheat; to seek justice, freedom, and plenty for all people;

9 to keep my tongue from lying, slandering, and harmful gossip, and never by my silence to let others be wrongly condemned;

10 to be thankful and generous; to do my duty cheerfully, and not to be greedy or envious.

Thus I acknowledge God's reign among people and try to live as a citizen of his kingdom, fighting against evil wherever I find it, in myself, or in the world around me.

V. THE HOLY SPIRIT IN THE CHURCH

Grace

26 *How can you carry out these duties and overcome temptation and sin?*
I can do these things only by the help of God and through his grace.

27 *What do you mean by God's grace?*
By God's grace I mean that God himself acts in Jesus Christ to forgive, inspire, and strengthen me by his Holy Spirit.

28 *In what ways do you receive these gifts of God's grace?*
I receive these gifts of God's grace within the fellowship of the Church, when I worship and pray, when I read the Bible, when I receive the Sacraments, and as I live my daily life to his glory.

Worship and Prayer

29   *What do you mean by the worship of God?*
     To worship God is to respond to his love, first by joining in the
     Church's offering of praise, thanksgiving, and prayer, and by
     hearing his holy word; secondly by acknowledging him as Lord of
     my life, and by doing my work for his honour and glory.

30   *Why do we keep Sunday as the chief day of public worship?*
     We keep Sunday as the chief day of public worship because it was
     on the first day of the week that our Lord Jesus Christ rose from
     the dead.

31   *What is prayer?*
     Prayer is the lifting up of heart and mind to God. We adore him,
     we confess our sins and ask to be forgiven, we thank him, we pray
     for others and for ourselves, we listen to him and seek to know
     his will.

32   *Repeat the Lord's Prayer.*
     Our Father in heaven,
     hallowed be your name,
     your kingdom come,
     your will be done,
     on earth as in heaven.
     Give us today our daily bread.
     Forgive us our sins
     as we forgive those who sin against us.
     Lead us not into temptation
     but deliver us from evil.
     For the kingdom, the power,
     and the glory are yours
     now and for ever.
     Amen.

     (or)

Our Father, who art in heaven,
hallowed be thy name;
thy kingdom come;
thy will be done;
on earth as it is in heaven.
Give us this day our daily bread.
And forgive us our trespasses,
as we forgive those who trespass against us.
And lead us not into temptation;
but deliver us from evil.
For thine is the kingdom,
the power and the glory,
for ever and ever.
Amen.

The Bible

33 *What is the Bible?*
    The Bible, in both the Old and the New Testaments, is the record
    of God's revelation of himself to humankind through his people
    Israel, and above all in his Son, Jesus Christ.

34 *How was the Bible given to us?*
    The Bible was given to us by the Holy Spirit who first inspired
    and guided the writers, and then led the Church to accept their
    writings as Holy Scripture.

35 *How should we read the Bible?*
    We should read the Bible with the desire and prayer that through
    it God will speak to us by his Holy Spirit, and enable us to know
    him and do his will.

The Gospel Sacraments and other Ministries of Grace

36 *What do you mean by a sacrament?*
By a sacrament I mean the use of material things as signs and pledges of God's grace, and as a means by which we receive his gifts.

37 *What are the two parts of a sacrament?*
The two parts of a sacrament are the outward and visible sign, and the inward and spiritual grace.

38 *How many sacraments has Christ, in the Gospel, appointed for his Church?*
Christ in the Gospel has appointed two sacraments for his Church, as needed by all for fullness of life, Baptism, and Holy Communion.

39 *What other sacramental ministries of grace are provided in the Church?*
Other sacramental ministries of grace are confirmation, ordination, holy matrimony, the ministry of absolution, and the ministry of healing.

40 *What is **Baptism**?*
Baptism is the sacrament in which, through the action of the Holy Spirit, we are 'christened' or made Christ's.

41 *What is the outward and visible sign in Baptism?*
The outward and visible sign in Baptism is water in which the person is baptized *In the Name of the Father, and of the Son, and of the Holy Spirit.*

42 *What is the inward and spiritual gift in Baptism?*
The inward and spiritual gift in Baptism is union with Christ in his death and resurrection, the forgiveness of sins, and a new birth into God's family, the Church.

43 *What is required of persons to be baptized?*
It is required that persons to be baptized should turn from sin, believe the Christian Faith, and give themselves to Christ to be his servants.

44 *Why then are infants baptized?*
Infants are baptized because, though they are not yet old enough to make the promises for themselves, others, making the promises for them, can claim their adoption as children of God.

45 *What is **Confirmation**?*
Confirmation is the ministry by which, through prayer with the laying on of hands by the Bishop, the Holy Spirit is received to complete what he began in Baptism, and to give strength for the Christian life.

46 *What is required of persons to be confirmed?*
It is required that persons to be confirmed should have been baptized, be sufficiently instructed in the Christian Faith, be penitent for their sins, and be ready to confess Jesus Christ as Saviour and obey him as Lord.

47 *What is **Holy Communion**?*
Holy Communion is the sacrament in which, according to Christ's command, we make continual remembrance of him, his passion, death, and resurrection, until his coming again, and in which we thankfully receive the benefits of his sacrifice.

It is, therefore, called the Eucharist, the Church's sacrifice of praise and thanksgiving; and also the Lord's Supper, the meal of fellowship which unites us to Christ and to the whole Church.

48 *What is the outward and visible sign in Holy Communion?*
The outward and visible sign in Holy Communion is bread and wine given and received as the Lord commanded.

49 *What is the inward and spiritual gift in Holy Communion?*
The inward and spiritual gift in Holy Communion is the Body and Blood of Christ, truly and indeed given by him and received by the faithful.

50 *What is meant by receiving the Body and Blood of Christ?*
Receiving the Body and Blood of Christ means receiving the life of Christ himself, who was crucified and rose again, and is now alive for evermore.

51 *What are the benefits we receive in Holy Communion?*
The benefits we receive are the strengthening of our union with Christ and his Church, the forgiveness of our sins, and the nourishing of ourselves for eternal life.

52 *What is required of those who come to Holy Communion?*
It is required of those who come to Holy Communion that they have a living faith in God's mercy through Christ, with a thankful remembrance of his death and resurrection; that they repent truly of their sins, intending to lead the new life; and be in charity with all people.

53 *What is **Ordination**?*
Ordination is the ministry in which, through prayer with the laying on of hands, our Lord Jesus Christ gives the grace of the Holy Spirit, and authority, to those who are being made bishops, priests, and deacons.

54 *What is **Holy Matrimony**?*
Holy Matrimony is Christian marriage, in which the man and the woman, entering into a life-long union, take their vows before God and seek his grace and blessing to fulfil them.

55　*What is the ministry of **Absolution**?*
The ministry of absolution is the ministry by which those who are truly sorry for their sins, and have made free confession of them to God in the presence of the minister, with intention to amend their lives, receive through him the forgiveness of God.

56　*What is the sacramental ministry of **Healing**?*
The sacramental ministry of healing is the ministry by which God's grace is given for the healing of spirit, mind and body, in response to faith and prayer, by the laying on of hands, or by anointing with oil.

VI. THE CHRISTIAN HOPE

57　*What is the hope in which a Christian lives?*
A Christian lives in the certain hope of the advent of Christ, the last judgement, and resurrection to life everlasting.

58　*What are we to understand by the advent of Christ?*
By the advent of Christ we are to understand that God, who through Christ has created and redeemed all things, will also through Christ at his coming again, make all things perfect and complete in his eternal kingdom.

59　*What are we to understand by the last judgement?*
By the last judgement we are to understand that all people will give account of their lives to God, who will condemn and destroy all that is evil, and bring his servants into the joy of their Lord.

60　*What are we to understand by resurrection?*
By resurrection we are to understand that God, who has overcome death by the resurrection of Christ, will raise from death in a body of glory all who are Christ's, that they may live with him in the fellowship of the saints.

61 *What, then, is our assurance as Christians?*
Our assurance as Christians is that neither death, nor life, nor things present, nor things to come, shall be able to separate us from the love of God which is in Christ Jesus our Lord. Thus, daily increasing in God's Holy Spirit, and following the example of our Saviour Christ, we shall at the last be made like unto him, for we shall see him as he is.

Therefore I pray:

May the God of all grace, who has called us unto his eternal glory by Christ Jesus, after that we have suffered awhile, make us perfect, stablish, strengthen, settle us.
To him be glory and dominion for ever and ever.

The Revised Catechism was drawn up by the Archbishops' Commission to Revise the Church Catechism. It was commended for use in teaching first by the Convocations of Canterbury and York and since 1973 by the General Synod of the Church of England. The most recent extension of the period of commendation is from 1 January 1996 until discontinued by resolution of the Synod.

The authors of *Pilgrim* have made light revisions to *The Revised Catechism* for this Guide in consultation with the Faith and Order Commission of the House of Bishops. The revisions have been to make the language of the Catechism inclusive and to use contemporary forms of liturgical texts in line with *Common Worship*.

pilgrim

PART FIVE:
AND FINALLY ...

Three Images of the Catechist

St Paul writes extensively about the work of growing new Christians in 1 Corinthians 3. In this chapter the apostles use three interlocking images to present the role of the catechist in the growth and life of those who are coming to faith. Each image is deeply rooted in the biblical tradition of teaching and learning the faith.

The first is the image of the parent:

> And so brothers and sisters, I could not speak to you as spiritual people but rather as people of the flesh, as infants in Christ. I fed you with milk, not solid food.
>
> I CORINTHIANS 3.1

This image of the parent emphasizes the deep bonds of love between those who are called to teach the faith and those who are learning the faith. It communicates the need for gentleness and nurture and for particular care to be given to nourish those who are new to faith.

The second image is that of gardeners or farmers working together to see the harvest:

> I planted, Apollos watered, but God gave the growth. So neither the one who plants nor the one who waters is anything but only God who gives the growth. The one who plants and the one who waters have a common purpose and each will receive wages according to the labours of each. For we are God's servants working together; you are God's field, God's building.
>
> 1 CORINTHIANS 3.6–9

This image emphasizes the regular, seasonal nature of catechesis in the life of the Church. We should be sowing the seed of the gospel, planting and watering and seeing a harvest of people brought into the kingdom of God on a regular basis (Matthew 9.37). The image emphasizes collaboration: this is not the work of a single minister but of ministers working together each with different tasks. The image emphasizes also the dedication and hard work required in the task before us.

The third image is one of building:

> According to the grace of God given to me, like a skilled master builder I laid a foundation and someone else is building on it. Each builder must choose with care how to build on it. For no one can lay any foundation other than the one that has been laid; that foundation is Jesus Christ.
>
> 1 CORINTHIANS 3.10–11

Again the image speaks of steady, skilled work and of different roles within the overall task of making disciples. It speaks of the prime importance of centring our catechesis on the foundation of Jesus Christ. Yet there is another important element introduced into this image.

The builder to whom Paul hands on this work as the architect or master builder is not another minister but the disciple themselves. Although we need the help of others to begin the Way and the support of the Body of Christ to continue in the Way, each one of us is the builder with prime responsibility for our own discipleship. We are building, with the support of the whole Church, God's temple.

This means that catechesis has as its end goal not only mature disciples but disciples who are able to take responsibility for their own Christian lives and vocation and to live out their discipleship in the world.

> O gracious and holy Father;
> give us wisdom to perceive you,
> diligence to seek you,
> patience to wait for you,
> eyes to behold you
> a heart to meditate upon you
> and a life to proclaim you,
> through the power of the Spirit
> of Jesus Christ our Lord
>
> BENEDICT OF NURSIA (C.550)

NOTES

Celebrating the Wider Community of the Church – The Presentation of the Four Texts: for separate short services to mark the handing over of the four texts in public worship, see *Common Worship: Christian Initiation*, page 40 and following pages © The Archbishops' Council 2006, Church House Publishing.
Catechism of the Catholic Church, Burns and Oates, 2000:
On page 20: paragraph 53.
On page 32: paragraph 426.
Catechesis and the Christian Year – Prayer: diagram on page 29 is taken from 'Growing the Body of Christ', the Diocese of Sheffield strategy document.
Common Worship: Christian Initiation, Church House Publishing, 2006:
On page 57: Welcome of Disciples on the Way of Faith, pp. 33–5.
On page 60: Call and Celebration of the Decision to be Baptized or Confirmed or to Affirm Baptismal Faith, pp. 37–9.
On page 63: Celebration after an Initiation Service outside the Parish, pp. 182–3.
On page 65: Affirmation of the Christian Way, p. 36.
The Revised Catechism © The Archbishops' Council 1999, Church House Publishing.